UNDER PRESSU

How to Handle Low Self-Esteem

by Patience Coster

W
FRANKLIN WATTS
LONDON·SYDNEY

First published in 2014 by Franklin Watts

Copyright © Arcturus Holdings Limited

Franklin Watts
338 Euston Road
London NW1 3BH

Franklin Watts Australia
Level 17/207 Kent Street, Sydney NSW 2000

Produced by Arcturus Publishing Limited,
26/27 Bickels Yard, 151–153 Bermondsey Street, London SE1 3HA

Editors: Rachel Minay and Joe Harris
Design: Emma Randall
Cover design: Emma Randall

Picture Credits
Shutterstock: cover (ostill), 3, 6 (Monkey Business Images), 7 (PHOTOCREO Michal Bednarek), 8 (Monkey Business Images), 9 (ejwhite), 10 (Monkey Business Images), 11 (Ariwasabi), 12 (Adam Tinney), 13 (Vladimir Wrangel), 15 (PKruger), 15 (Stuart Monk), 16 (littleny), 17 (Monkey Business Images), 18 (oliveromg), 19 (Dudarev Mikhail), 20 (Monkey Business Images), 21 (LoloStock), 22 (Andrey_Popov), 23 (CREATISTA), 24 (Suzanne Tucker), 25 (Monkey Business Images), 26 (bikeriderlondon), 27 (Vitchanan Photography), 28 (Tadas_Naujokaitis), 29 (Vezzani Photography), 30 (Tyler Olson), 31 (mangostock), 32 (iofoto), 33 (Golden Pixels LLC), 34 (Samuel Borges Photography), 33 (Tarasov), 36 (CLS Design), 37 (Maxim Blinkov), 38 (AnneMS), 39 (Anastasija Popova), 40 (Monkey Business Images), 41 (Kerry Garvey), 42 (swinner), 43 (luminaimages).

A CIP catalogue record for this book is available from the British Library.

Dewey Decimal Classification Number 158.1

ISBN 978 1 4451 3241 9

Printed in China

Franklin Watts is a division of Hachette Children's Books, an Hachette UK company.
www.hachette.co.uk

SL004071UK

Supplier 29, Date 0514, Print Run 3393

CONTENTS

WHAT IS SELF-ESTEEM?

Self-esteem is what we feel we are worth and how much we feel other people value us. Healthy self-esteem means that we have a positive image of ourselves; it also means we believe that other people will like us for who we are. Self-esteem is important because it affects our mental health and the way we behave.

People with healthy self-esteem feel good about themselves, as well as loved, accepted and valued by others.

EMOTIONAL ARMOUR

Healthy self-esteem is a person's emotional armour against the challenges of the world. People who feel good about themselves seem to find it easier to handle conflicts and resist negative pressures. They tend to smile more readily and enjoy life.

NEGATIVE EMOTIONS

A person with low self-esteem has a negative self-image. This often affects how the person thinks other people see him or her. Although it is not a personal fault, people with low self-esteem often blame themselves and lack confidence.

SELF-ESTEEM AND YOUNG PEOPLE

Teenage years are full of changes and challenges, so healthy self-esteem is an important quality. It can help with a young person's schoolwork and social life, and may have an impact on his or her future experiences. But low self-esteem can make it difficult for a young person to cope with life's challenges.

Low self-esteem can lead to self-destructive behaviour such as binge drinking.

MENTAL-HEALTH ISSUES

Low self-esteem can make young people prone to mental-health problems such as **eating disorders**, **depression, anxiety** and **phobias**. It can also lead to a range of **reckless** and **antisocial** behaviours. However, low self-esteem is not something you are born with and stuck with; it is something lots of people experience and something you can change.

'I was terrified of failing'

I used to be an A* student — I always thought I'd go to university. But when I was about 14, I started feeling anxious and depressed. I found it really hard to concentrate on schoolwork because I was terrified of failing. I actually became afraid to do anything because I thought I'd never do it right. My mum tried to help, but whatever she said to try to boost my confidence, I just didn't believe it. In the end, she spoke to the school and they referred me to a counsellor. The counsellor was great — and really helped me feel better about myself. She said that even little things — like getting out of bed in the morning — were a big achievement for someone with depression.

WHAT CAUSES LOW SELF-ESTEEM?

Some of us may be born having a more positive outlook than others, but our self-esteem is also affected by our experiences in life. Negative experiences in childhood, combined with rejection and excessive pressure, may result in a young person developing low self-esteem.

EARLY EXPERIENCES

Young children look to their carers for emotional responses. If the response is kind, loving and happy, then children are likely to feel good about themselves. But children who get consistently negative responses may receive the message that they are, for example, 'stupid' or 'naughty', and will often develop low self-esteem.

Growing up in a happy, attentive and caring environment helps to build healthy self-esteem.

UNREALISTIC EXPECTATIONS

When adults place unrealistic expectations on children, it can trigger self-esteem issues. Young people who are constantly criticized, for getting poor results at school, for example, often learn to doubt themselves.

REJECTION

Any young person who experiences rejection – for example, not being chosen for the school choir or the basketball team – will probably feel a dip in confidence. Most people will manage to bounce back from such a setback. But a young person who has already experienced a lot of rejection may not be so **resilient**.

An unhappy, stressful and neglectful environment can lead to low self-esteem, especially if adults involve children in their problems.

TOO MUCH PRESSURE

Pressures such as bullying, childhood **trauma** or parents going through a divorce can cause young people to develop self-esteem issues. They may feel responsible even though it is not their fault. Young people who have been neglected may feel unimportant. On the other hand, those who have been overprotected may have low self-esteem because they have not developed the confidence to try things out for themselves.

Under Pressure Q&A

Why does my sister make me feel bad?

My older sister is always criticizing me. I think she does it to make herself feel good, but it makes me feel so small. Am I overreacting?

If your sister's words cause you to have a low opinion of yourself, you are not overreacting. Siblings often vie for position, but it becomes problematic if one sibling bullies another over a long period of time. Don't remain silent. Talk to someone you trust and ask for their help. Your sister's behaviour needs to be recognized for what it is – and challenged – so she can see that what she is doing is wrong.

9

THE TEENAGE YEARS

The teenage years are a time of great physical and emotional upheaval. These changes, combined with the desire to fit in with your peer group, can sometimes feel overwhelming. However exciting the journey towards adulthood may be, discovering who you are can be a painful and confusing process.

Some people struggle with their self-esteem and body image when they go through **puberty**.

CHANGES AND CHALLENGES

As a young person journeying through **adolescence**, you are confronted with many pressures. These include huge changes to your body shape combined with sexual feelings, a search for your own identity and a changing relationship with your parents.

SCHOOL LIFE

Young people are also under pressure to perform well at school, be sporty, have loads of friends and compete in the dating game. No wonder their confidence can be fragile! Low self-esteem can affect both teenage boys and teenage girls.

Girls may find that their self-esteem is particularly fragile while their body develops.

PEER PRESSURE

Young people may feel under pressure to 'fit in' with their friends – to feel accepted and safe in a crowd. Peer pressure can sometimes be positive – for example, it can give us the courage to try things we might not attempt on our own – but it can also make us do things that go against what we believe is right. If you have low self-esteem, you may compare yourself unfavourably with others and do things you feel uncomfortable with just to please the group.

OLD WOUNDS

Young people who had an unsettled time as a baby or toddler may discover that feelings of low self-esteem surface when they become teenagers. The feelings of insecurity may not have affected them during their early childhood, so their emergence can be frightening.

'I just wanted to be in the cool group'

I wanted to be like the boys in the 'cool' group at school. When one of them started making fun of a quiet girl in our class, I joined in. I didn't like myself for doing it, but I was afraid the other boys would make fun of me if I didn't. Anyway, there's a girl I like in my class and she asked me why I was being so horrible. I tried to make a joke about some of the geeky girls in school, but she didn't laugh. I couldn't give her a straight answer — I felt like an idiot for just following the group.

BODY IMAGE

Body image is how you view your physical self – whether you feel you are attractive, both to yourself and others. For young people, body image can be closely linked to self-esteem. How they feel about their bodies can spill over into other areas of their lives and potentially lower their self-esteem.

ANXIETY

Most young people experience anxiety over their appearance. At worst, their worries can make them feel like outcasts. A young person may fix on a physical feature he or she thinks is unattractive and build up a negative self-image in his or her mind.

SELF-CRITICAL

Real issues, such as a birthmark, outbreaks of spots or a scar can also contribute to low self-esteem. All the **hormonal** changes brought on by puberty can make young people highly self-conscious about issues like these.

Girls with low self-esteem may feel even more insecure when they see 'perfect' body images, which are achieved through methods such as airbrushing photos of models in magazines.

UNREAL MEDIA IMAGES

Young people often compare their changing bodies to peers and to **airbrushed** images of models in TV ads and magazines. Trying to meet these impossible and unreal standards of beauty can undermine a young person's self-confidence.

WEIGHT

As young people's bodies develop and grow, they will almost certainly gain weight. This, too, can have an impact on self-esteem. Girls may feel they are not slim enough, whereas boys may worry that they don't look muscular or strong enough. The important thing to remember is that not everyone grows or develops at the same time or in the same way.

Under Pressure Q&A

How can I stop feeling so ugly?

I worry that people think I'm ugly and laugh at me behind my back. What can I do to stop feeling so bad about myself?

As a young person, your body is going through lots of changes that can feel overwhelming. Some young people are hyper-critical of themselves and it sounds like you are one of them! Instead of focusing on the negatives, how about looking at your positive features? Are you a loyal friend? What subjects at school are you good at? Think about the things you like to do and keep on doing them. Don't give up! Your achievements will improve your self-esteem. If you feel good about yourself, others will too.

Boys' self-esteem can suffer if they fail to measure up to impossible camera- and computer-tweaked standards of masculinity.

FOOD-RELATED ISSUES

If you have low self-esteem, you may find fault with the way you look and try to 'fix the problem' by going on a crash diet. This can result in an unhealthy attitude to food.

EATING DISORDERS

Young people with low self-esteem may have a reckless and unhealthy attitude to food and are particularly at risk of developing eating disorders. A small number of girls and boys may develop full-blown eating disorders such as **anorexia nervosa** or **bulimia**.

WORRIES ABOUT WEIGHT

A recent survey revealed that 61 per cent of 11–13 year olds say they worry about their weight and 41 per cent admit that they have been on a diet. Among children under the age of ten, 28 per cent say they have been bullied because of their weight.

A significant number of young people have unhealthy dieting habits.

14

MODERN LIFE

Young people are under constant pressure to keep up with the latest trends and to look and act a certain way. Online social networking may be a good way to increase your circle of 'friends', but it also gives bullies a platform from which to taunt people **anonymously** about the way they look.

BEING THIN

The media bombards young people with false images, which reinforce the notion that being thin is the ideal. Not surprisingly, young people get the message that being thin makes you popular, successful and/or beautiful.

'Anorexia made me really ill'

I was diagnosed with anorexia nervosa when I was 14. I'd already crash-dieted for some time, but was never happy with the way I looked. I started monitoring all my food and each day tried to eat fewer and fewer calories. I kept losing weight, but still thought I looked fat. My mum told me how lovely I was, but I didn't listen to her. Eventually, I got a stomach bug and became really ill — it was scary. My mum took me to the doctor who said that anorexia had weakened my body's immune system. At last, I allowed my mum to contact a local clinic and book an assessment. They were really supportive and helpful — and now I'm on the road to recovery.

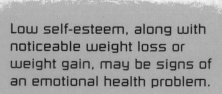

Low self-esteem, along with noticeable weight loss or weight gain, may be signs of an emotional health problem.

SCHOOL LIFE

Much of teenage life revolves around school. Young people with low self-esteem can find it very hard to cope with the pressures of school. Low self-esteem can affect a young person's academic performance and social life. It can also make him or her a target for bullies.

Young people with healthy self-esteem see the results of their hard work and try to succeed because they believe they can.

SCHOOL WORK

A young person with low self-esteem may say things like 'I'm stupid' or 'I can't do that' (before he or she has tried). This can lead to a vicious circle, where the young person stops trying to succeed academically and then feels bad about it. This can lead to depression.

FRIENDSHIPS

Young people with low self-esteem may have trouble making and keeping friends. They may feel as though they're not worthy of friendship. They may be uncomfortable talking with others or not be sure how to relate to them. If a young person feels he or she is not 'cool' or 'popular', this may have a further negative effect on his or her self-image.

BULLYING

Young people with low self-esteem can be withdrawn or shy and find it difficult to have fun. They are more likely to 'follow the herd' and more vulnerable to being bullied. Persistent bullying by peers can further damage their self-esteem.

Young people who are lacking in confidence may be vulnerable to bullying, which will further damage their sense of self.

Under Pressure Q&A

I hate school – what should I do?

My mates have decided they don't like me for some reason, my grades have slumped and I hate going to school. Mum and Dad are on my case about my work, but I can't tell them how terrible I feel. What should I do?

You need to start by screening out this negative 'noise' and focusing on your good qualities – yes, you definitely have them! Find someone you can trust to talk to, if not face to face, then maybe online or via a helpline. Pinpoint why you dislike school – are your classmates the main problem, is it the schoolwork, or is it both? Think about things you enjoy doing. Is there a club you could join? Or maybe you'd prefer to do something on your own, like art, writing or learning an instrument? Make a list of possible options, get some reliable support and focus on restoring some balance to your life.

BEHAVIOURAL CHOICES

As a young person, it is normal to have rebellious feelings and to debate your ideas at length — sometimes passionately! This is all part of discovering who you are and what you believe. But young people with healthy self-esteem express their individuality in a very different way from those with low self-esteem.

Young people with low self-esteem often take their negative feelings out on others through bullying.

COPING STRATEGIES

Most young people go through rebellious phases. Some young people with low self-esteem may be the victims of bullies, but others may themselves resort to negative behaviours, such as bullying, cheating, lying or avoiding school. They often take their negative emotions out on others to avoid feeling bad themselves.

CUTTING CLASS

Young people with low self-esteem are more likely to cut classes or join in with others who are also skipping school. They are less likely to take school study seriously and, as a result, may have poorer grades. They are more likely to take part in **disruptive** behaviour in class.

'We thought it was a real laugh'

I got on fine at school until I was 12, when my mum had another baby. Suddenly it was all about the baby and if I said anything against him, my mum got really upset and angry. I started getting into fights at school and pushing some of the younger kids in the playground around. A couple of mates suggested we started 'trolling' — posting abusive messages to one of the younger boys on a social networking site. We thought it was a real laugh. But then the boy's parents contacted the school. The head told us that our bullying would not be tolerated and had to stop immediately. We each had to write a letter apologizing to the boy we had bullied. As I wrote my letter, I started to see my bullying in a different light. I think I was bullying those other kids to make up for feeling bad about myself.

Young people with low self-esteem may be at higher risk of joining gangs and committing crimes.

AGGRESSION

The worse a young person behaves, the more negative feedback he or she gets. This makes the young person feel bad about him or herself. Young people who fall into this cycle may act aggressively in order to feel superior to others and boost their sense of self-worth.

SUBSTANCE ABUSE AND SELF-HARMING

Some young people feel as if nothing bad could ever happen to them and are willing to take certain risks. They may engage in reckless activities such as binge-drinking alcohol, taking drugs, having unprotected sex or self-harming. This self-destructive behaviour is sometimes brought about by low self-esteem.

TEENAGE KICKS?

Young people with low self-esteem may turn to alcohol to try to boost their confidence and improve their social skills, at least temporarily. Young people who suffer from low self-esteem are also more likely to engage in reckless behaviour such as having unprotected sex or taking drugs. They may believe that risky sex, drugs and alcohol will quiet their negative thoughts and help them cope with daily living.

Young people who are harassed via email, social networking sites or other online forums are twice as likely as other adolescents to become substance abusers.

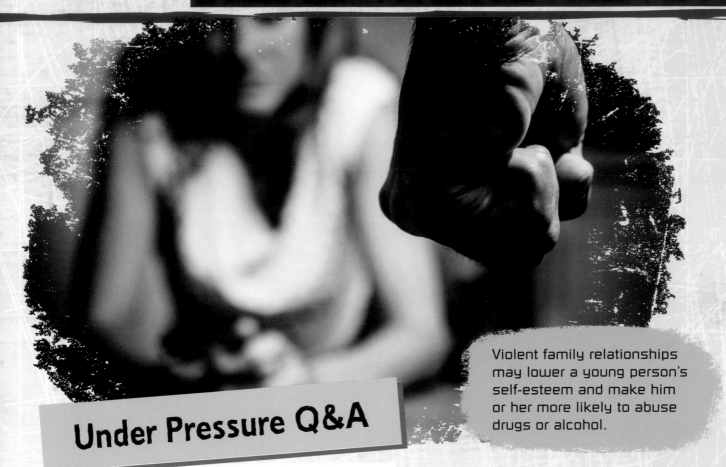

Violent family relationships may lower a young person's self-esteem and make him or her more likely to abuse drugs or alcohol.

Under Pressure Q&A

Should I just not go?

I am going to stay at my best friend's place overnight as her parents are away. Her boyfriend and some other friends will be there. They like to drink alcohol, but I don't. How can I get through the night without looking like a killjoy? Or should I just not go?

Just because you don't want to drink alcohol doesn't mean you should miss out on an evening with your friends. But you need to be assertive, so you don't spend the evening being 'worn down' by their efforts to get you to drink. Practise saying 'No' in a polite but firm way – 'No, thanks. Alcohol's not really my thing.' If they are good friends, they will not keep trying to make you do things you don't want to do. Equally, if the idea of going makes you feel unsafe or unhappy, it would be better not to go.

SELF-HARM

Similarly, young people who find it difficult to talk about their feelings may turn to self-harming. Forms of self-harm include cutting, scratching, burning, pulling hair and skin, and head banging.

ABUSE

Young people who have been victims of physical, sexual or emotional abuse are at greater risk of turning to substance abuse and self-harming. If young people are helped to develop a sense of self-worth, they may think twice before resorting to self-destructive behaviour.

21

FAMILY LIFE

Young people who are constantly criticized or ignored by their parents or siblings may develop low self-esteem. So too may young people who are under a lot of pressure to succeed, or who are going through traumas such as parental separation or divorce.

The home should be a place of refuge after the rough and tumble of school. But sometimes stresses within the family can affect a young person's self-esteem.

UNKIND TEASING

Persistent, unkind teasing by family members can cause low self-esteem. In general, family members are most likely to act badly towards one another if they feel bad about themselves. This creates a cycle of unhappiness – the worse they treat others, the worse they get treated in return.

Talk to a family member about your concerns and fears. Choose a time when they're not busy or distracted by something else and can really listen to what you want to say.

UNREALISTIC PRESSURE

Family members who are dissatisfied with themselves may place unrealistic pressure on young people to look or behave a certain way. Young people who fail to live up to this image may then become withdrawn and negative. They may even give up trying because they feel they will never be good enough.

SEPARATION AND DIVORCE

When parents separate, it's a stressful and hurtful time for everyone involved. A young person's self-esteem can suffer as he or she struggles to keep up with schoolwork while dealing with arguing parents, reduced family finances and perhaps a change in home and school.

'Making the hurt worse'

My dad left when I was 13. After that, I spent a lot of time being angry with Mum and winding up my sisters. I suppose I was really mad at Dad, because I thought he didn't care about us. One day my mum got really upset, and then I felt so bad — I started to think that he left because of me. Mum said this wasn't true and that it was completely normal for me to feel angry and upset. But she also told me that to criticize myself, when I was already hurting, only made the hurt worse. She said it was important for me to treat myself well, not badly. During the next few months, I started to be less hard on myself and found it a bit easier to control my angry feelings.

ABUSE

Young people who have been abused – neglected, punished harshly or **molested** – from an early age will probably struggle with their self-esteem. Without meaning to, they may repeat the cycle of violence they had no control over when they were younger.

RIPPLE EFFECT

Children who have been abused may be unable to distinguish between acceptable and unacceptable behaviour. They run a significant risk of being caught up in a ripple effect and finding themselves in abusive relationships as teens and adults.

LACK OF TRUST

Children who have not been protected by the adults they trusted are unlikely to have trust in anyone else's ability to protect or help them. As they grow up, they may make poor choices of friends and partners, which could leave them open to further abuse.

Neglect or ill-treatment in the early years of a child's life may lead to a belief that her or his needs are unimportant.

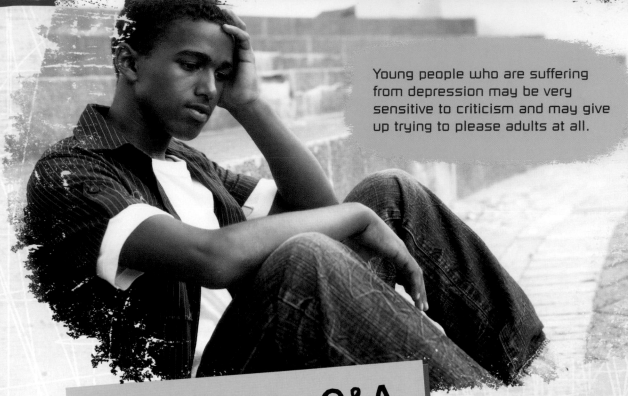

Young people who are suffering from depression may be very sensitive to criticism and may give up trying to please adults at all.

Under Pressure Q&A

How should I cope with my dad's anger?

When my dad gets angry, he brings up everything I've ever done wrong. He makes me feel worthless. What's the best way to cope?

Whether your dad is telling you off for something you have done wrong, or dumping his own negative feelings on you, he needs to understand the effect of his behaviour. Choose a moment when he is calm and try to explain how bad he makes you feel. Try to tell him that you understand he wants to inspire you to be a better person, but his current method is having the opposite effect. It is making you lose confidence and self-respect. If you can't talk to your dad face to face, ask a trusted member of your family to speak to him on your behalf or, if this is not possible, seek help outside the family.

FUTURE PROBLEMS

Young people who have been abused by those supposed to care for them may place themselves in situations that are unsafe, have difficulty forming long-term, trusting relationships or have body-image issues.

NEGLECT

A young person who has been neglected as a child may feel that he or she is unimportant and unlovable, which could lead to poor behaviour. It could also mean that he or she has difficulty maintaining healthy relationships and may lead to mental-health problems.

A LONG-TERM PROBLEM

Low self-esteem is a thinking disorder. Once formed, it can colour every thought a young person has. If a young person can't see solutions to daily problems, he or she may feel stressed, anxious and unhappy.

'I CAN'T'

Young people with low self-esteem can find new challenges a source of major anxiety and frustration. Their immediate response may be: 'I can't.' They may speak negatively about themselves, saying things such as: 'I'll never learn how to do this,' or 'What's the point? Nobody cares about me anyway.'

NOT GOOD ENOUGH?

Teenage girls are particularly prone to feelings of low self-esteem. According to recent studies, seven out of ten girls think they are not good enough in some way. They don't believe they measure up in terms of their looks, their performance at school, their friendships or their relationships with family members.

Children with healthy self-esteem are resilient enough to cope with new challenges and experiences.

If young people are given to self-critical thoughts such as 'I'm no good' or 'I can't do anything right', they may become passive, withdrawn or depressed.

NEGATIVE ACTIVITIES

There seems to be a link between low self-esteem and an increased risk of teenage pregnancy. Also, 75 per cent of girls with low self-esteem report taking part in negative activities such as cutting, bullying, smoking, drinking or disordered eating. By contrast, 25 per cent of girls with healthy self-esteem report engaging in such activities. But whatever the statistics say, one thing is clear – the damage done to self-esteem in young people, if left unrepaired, is difficult to undo later on in life.

'My foster parents were there for me'

When I was a baby, I was taken away from my biological mum because she couldn't look after me. I went through five different homes before I was four, when I moved to a permanent **foster home**. But by the time I was 12, I had started skipping school, shoplifting and getting into other kinds of trouble, and I was moved to a children's home. To begin with, I felt alone and empty, but soon I got to know other kids and discovered that they had been through similar things. I realized I wasn't alone. But I also realized that in spite of my difficult start in life, my foster parents had been there for me. What I would say to others like me is: there is hope, and there are great people who can support you.

THE POWER OF POSITIVE THINKING

Do you think you're no good? Do you put yourself down?
If so, you're not alone. It's not always easy to like everything
about yourself, but when you get stuck on the negatives it
can really lower your self-esteem.

If you believe you are
unattractive, make a note
of when you receive a
compliment from someone
who says you look good or
they like your new haircut.

ELIMINATE THE NEGATIVE

To start improving your self-esteem, you have to understand your negative
beliefs. Are they to do with how you look, your abilities or your personality?
Do you remember when you started to feel like this? Can you identify an
experience that might have caused it?

MAKE A LIST

Once you have identified your negative beliefs, gather evidence to challenge
them. Write down things you like about yourself so that you have a list to
refer to when you are feeling low.

ACCENTUATE THE POSITIVE

Think about your best feature and write it down — for example 'I like my hair', 'I'm good at music', 'I'm a loyal friend'. Think about things you have achieved and add them to the list. This list is good to refer to when you are having a bad day or are nervous about something, such as an exam.

KNOW YOURSELF

Remember how important it is to be positive about yourself. People with healthy self-esteem know themselves well. They're realistic and find friends who like and appreciate them for who they are. They usually feel more in control of their lives and understand their strengths and weaknesses.

Think about nice things you have done for other people, skills you have, talents that you or others have noticed and write all these positive things down.

Under Pressure Q&A

Why do I feel self-conscious all the time?

It may sound mad, but I'm afraid of being noticed. Sometimes, my legs tremble just when I'm walking down the street! What's wrong with me?

It's natural to feel self-conscious, nervous or shy at times. It is not an illness — it's very common in young people, and usually it will pass. But there are steps you can take to help yourself. Strange as it may seem, you need to build your confidence by going beyond what feels comfortable for you — little by little. New things may seem daunting, but once you've done them you will feel more confident and each small step forwards will help you build enough confidence to take the next small step. You may need to ask family, friends or a therapist to help with this. But remember — keep practising and don't give up.

BEING YOUR OWN BEST FRIEND

Once you have started to retrain your 'inner critic' and stopped putting yourself down, you can work on becoming your own best friend. By making time for yourself and valuing yourself, you will begin to improve your self-esteem.

Young people with healthy self-esteem know they have positive traits that others will appreciate. They can work through conflicts with others. This skill will serve them well as they go through life.

TAKING CARE OF YOURSELF

Start by thinking how to make your life a more positive experience. School can be stressful. If you are spending too much time outside school on extra-curricular activities or a job, you may be spreading yourself too thinly. Re-evaluate your schedule so that it is more manageable for you, and be sure to include enough time for relaxation, time with family and friends – and sleep!

RELAX

Be kind to yourself and use relaxation to help your mind and body switch off from life's pressures. Breathe slowly and deeply to help your body relax. Have a warm bath, listen to music or read a book. Take up an activity unrelated to school. Often, when you go back to the thing you were finding stressful, you can cope better if you have taken a break from it.

It's official: doing good feels good! Scientists have found that people who volunteer for causes they care about tend to be happier and healthier, and even live longer.

CHOOSE RELATIONSHIPS WITH CARE

Look at the people around you and think about how they make you feel. If you are spending a lot of time with someone who makes you feel bad about yourself, then spend less time with them and more time with people who make you feel good about yourself.

DOING GOOD MAKES YOU FEEL GOOD

If you do things you feel proud of, it can help you to feel better about yourself. You could do a sponsored event or become a volunteer. Voluntary work enables you to do some good and meet new people who may share the same values as you.

'I thought I wasn't good-looking enough'

I really liked Jade, but I thought I wasn't good-looking enough to ask her out. My mate Luke told me that most girls are interested in more than just looks. They want a guy to have good qualities like kindness and a sense of humour. I talked to one of my older cousins about it and she suggested I started by relaxing, going for long walks and taking time over my personal grooming. Gradually I started to feel more confident and more okay about my looks. Then I thought, 'What's the worst that can happen?' — and I asked Jade out. She said yes!

TALKING IT THROUGH

If your self-esteem is low, it can help to talk about your feelings to a friend or family member. People close to you are more likely to be sensitive to changes in your mood. You might feel that they won't understand, but they may surprise you.

Talk to someone you trust – explain how you are feeling and any concerns you may have.

REACHING OUT

In most cases, friends and family will want to help if they can. Who do you find it easiest to talk to about personal matters? Choose someone who's a good listener and who won't judge you.

TRUST

Be sure to pick someone you trust. If it's a friend, try to choose someone you have known for a while, since they are more likely to have a better picture of you than someone you have known for just a short period of time.

EMOTIONAL SUPPORT

Pick a time and place where you can have a conversation properly without being interrupted. Choose somewhere quiet where you will be able to concentrate. Explain how you are feeling and what you think this person can do to help.

You may feel that adults won't understand, but they might have experienced difficult times or feelings of low self-worth themselves and be able to offer support.

IN CONFIDENCE

Make it clear that you don't want the person you are confiding in to gossip about your conversation. You need to be sure that your innermost feelings are respected. However, if your problem is health-threatening, the person will need to tell a responsible adult for your own safety.

Under Pressure Q&A

How can I face a crowd of people?

I was bullied for two years in school. The bullying has stopped but I still find myself believing what the bullies said — that I am weak and ugly. A friend has asked me to go to a party with her, but how can I face a room full of people who will judge me?

Your friend may have asked you to go along to keep her company, but she may also have picked up on your feelings and asked because she cares about you. If you trust her and feel you can talk to her, it would be worth discussing how you feel. Then maybe you could talk about going to the party together and looking out for each other while you are there. Although you will probably be nervous to begin with, you may even find you enjoy yourself!

THE FOOD–MOOD CONNECTION

There is increasing evidence of a link between what we eat and how we feel. This is called the 'food–mood' connection. Similarly, the way we feel influences what we choose to eat or drink.

YOU ARE WHAT YOU EAT

Foods that contain complex **carbohydrates**, such as wholegrains, beans and vegetables, provide us with **glucose**, the brain's main source of fuel. Without this fuel, we can't think clearly. Proteins found in meat, fish and soya products are also vital to good mental health. A lack of these nutrients can lead to feelings of depression, **apathy** or anxiety.

THE IMPORTANCE OF FATS

Essential fats, found mainly in oily fish, seeds and nuts, cannot be made within the body, so we need to get them from food. The brain is made up of 60 per cent fat, and the fats we eat directly affect its structure. A lack of 'healthy' fats has been linked to mental-health problems, including depression and lack of concentration.

Eating healthily affects the way you feel about yourself.

Try to only eat ready meals and takeaway food occasionally.

REGULAR MEALS

Try to eat three meals a day with two 'healthy' snacks (for example, fruit or yoghurt) in between. Make sure you have breakfast within an hour of waking up. Aim to have at least five portions of fruit and vegetables and drink plenty of water every day.

FOODS TO AVOID

If you consume lots of sugary foods, fizzy drinks and **stimulants** such as coffee, your blood-sugar levels go up suddenly, causing mood swings. You may become irritable, anxious or dizzy.

'I was tired and fed up all the time'

I was feeling tired and fed up all the time. The school nurse made an appointment with a nutritionist for me. The nutritionist explained that eating too many sugary and fast foods affects a person's mood, which in turn can affect confidence and self-esteem. He advised me to eat sensibly and to include foods such as green vegetables, nuts, seasonal fruits and yogurt in my diet, which would give me more energy over a longer period of time. I worked out a menu plan with my mum. After a couple of weeks, we both noticed that my mood had improved — and my skin was clearer too. Because I felt healthier, I started to feel more positive about life.

EXERCISE

Everyone knows that exercise is good for the body – but did you know that it's important for your mental health, too? Exercise helps your brain to release chemicals called **endorphins** that make you feel good. To keep feeling positive about yourself, aim to do **30** minutes of moderate exercise, five days a week.

WHAT KIND OF EXERCISE?

Exercise is a great way to raise self-esteem. Any exercise is good – find something you like to do that fits into your day. Moderate exercise means you're working hard enough to raise your heart rate and break a sweat, but not so out of breath that you can't talk. It includes things such as walking, swimming, dancing, riding your bike, skateboarding, rollerblading and walking to school instead of getting the bus (or getting off a few stops early).

RELAXATION

Yoga, tai chi and pilates are types of exercise that are designed around relaxation and breathing techniques. They are strengthening and confidence-building and can help with anxiety and stress.

SETTING GOALS

Exercise makes your body feel stronger and more balanced, which helps with confidence. You might find it useful to exercise with a friend, so that you can motivate each other. Set goals and measure your progress, so you can see the difference it makes.

Research shows that physical activity can be as good at lifting your mood as antidepressants or psychological treatments such as cognitive behavioural therapy (CBT).

Under Pressure Q&A

How can I focus on the good things?

When people compliment me, I'm still not satisfied. I focus on my flaws and it makes me feel horrible. What are some tips for focusing on the good and not the bad?

One of the best ways to focus on the good is through exercise. It can get you feeling more confident, both mentally and physically. If you start to feel down, try going for a run or a swim, or dancing round your room to your favourite music. You'll probably feel your mood lift and you might not focus on your flaws. Also, think about your good qualities and you'll realize there's much to be proud of, both inside and out.

Think about the type of activities you are interested in and build your exercise around that.

A FOUR-LEGGED FRIEND

Caring for a pet can help with low self-esteem. Pets offer unconditional love — they accept their owners as they are. A relationship with a pet is less complicated than a relationship with parents or peers. A pet won't judge you or tell you what to do!

Coming home to the affection of a dog can be a comfort for a young person with low self-esteem.

ANIMAL PRESENCE

Young people can really benefit from the presence of an animal in their lives. Focusing their energy on a pet such as a dog, cat, hamster or rabbit can help take their mind off other pressures and worries.

UNCONDITIONAL LOVE

A pet doesn't care what's cool, or how clever or 'popular' you are. A dog will be there to welcome its owner with a happy, wagging tail after a bad day at school. Its loyalty and friendship can help lessen feelings of loneliness and isolation.

POSITIVE FOCUS

By taking responsibility for the life of another creature and providing it with food, shelter, affection and entertainment, you will gain an awareness of your own value and importance.

EXERCISE AND MOTIVATION

You will find that daily walks with a dog can boost your spirits and help maintain a healthy body weight. Getting fresh air also helps you to relax and sleep better. And there is a reason to get out of bed in the morning, if a pet is depending on you.

Unlike your peers, pets don't care about what you look like or the clothes that you wear. They just want to be cared for and to have fun!

'All of a sudden, things don't seem so bad'

Sometimes I have a hard time at school. There's a group of boys there who tease me and call me 'gay'. Some days it's hard to get out of bed. But I'm so grateful I have my rescue dog, Jaz, to come home to. When I've had a bad day at school and all I feel like doing is curling up in a darkened room, Jaz comes dashing down the path to greet me. She always brings her squeaky toy for me to throw. All of a sudden, things don't seem so bad. If it's not raining, I'll usually grab my bike and take Jaz out for a run. Life's better with her by my side. One day, I'll find a person I feel close to — someone who loves me as much as Jaz does.

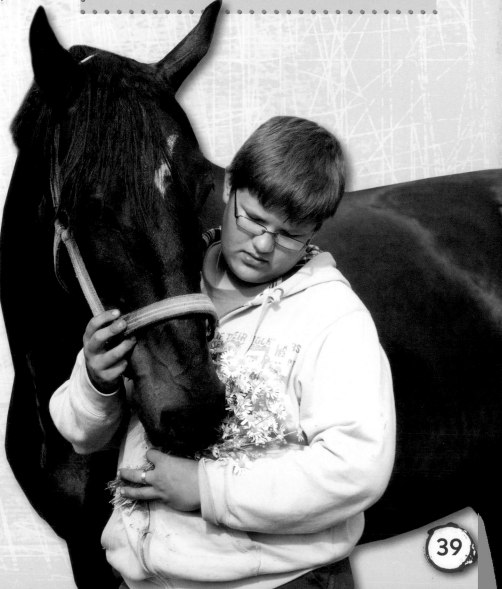

GETTING HELP

Some emotional hurts are too deep and long lasting to be overcome without the help of a mental-health professional. Therapists and counsellors can work with young people to identify coping strategies for dealing with problems at school or at home.

A counsellor can help a young person with low self-esteem to cope with problems and feel better about him or herself.

DANGER SIGNS

It is vital to healthy self-esteem to develop the confidence to understand when you can deal with a problem and when you need to ask for help. If your self-esteem is so low that you are suffering from depression, or you have lost interest in family or friends, developed an eating disorder or are taking part in dangerous behaviour such as using drugs, you probably need help from a guidance counsellor or therapist. Therapy can help you learn to view yourself and the world more positively and it can reveal ways of solving problems.

TALK IT THROUGH

If you are thinking of going for therapy, start by talking to someone you trust, such as your school counsellor. He or she may also be able to suggest an online forum where people are experiencing similar situations to you. Or, if you don't feel like talking to anyone face to face, you could phone a helpline.

Under Pressure Q&A

Am I crazy?

Does going for therapy mean I'm crazy? Will I feel uncomfortable talking about my problems?

Going for therapy does not mean you are crazy! At least one in five teens has mental-health issues and it is important and brave to seek help. It is normal to feel awkward talking about sensitive things, but this should get easier over time. The therapist will support you and suggest ways to approach problems so that you can sort them out yourself. It's important to have a good relationship with your therapist — if you don't feel you can talk easily to him or her, it is OK to try a different therapist.

If you can't think of anyone you feel comfortable talking with to face to face, there are helplines you can call to discuss your problems.

SAYING 'YES' TO LIFE

Overcoming self-esteem issues will help you face new experiences in a positive way. If you learn to view problems as a challenge rather than a threat, you can work towards solving them without putting yourself or others down. Healthy self-esteem will help you to experience each day with interest and enthusiasm — to say 'yes' to life.

Doing something that you enjoy, that you are good at, and that you can be proud of, will help you fight low self-esteem.

EMBRACE DIFFERENCE

Although young people are under a lot of pressure to 'follow the crowd', remember that it's fine to be different from your peers. You have your own unique path in life, so don't be overly influenced by the opinions of others — pursue your own dreams.

FIND OUT WHAT YOU ARE GOOD AT

It's important to put your thoughts in perspective and recognize that everyone has their own talents and strengths. For example, you may not be good at sports, but you may be good at music, working with animals, or cooking. Each of us is good at something!

LOVE WHO YOU ARE

Learning to understand and like yourself is at the heart of healthy self-esteem. While some people are naturally outgoing, others are more shy. Modern society may seem to value the chatty people, but without quiet types we would have few thinkers, inventors, writers and artists. The world needs both types of people!

KEEP SELF-TALK UPBEAT!

Overcoming negative self-talk is key to overcoming self-esteem issues. Use positive self-statements, such as: 'I am far too good to feel sorry for myself!' to nurture your self-esteem.

'My friend was always putting herself down'

My friend Kerry was always putting herself down. She would often give up on her schoolwork, saying that she just couldn't do it, and she never seemed to be happy about the way she looked. I told Kerry what a great friend she was and how she didn't need to be so self-critical because she is really clever and pretty. Kerry said she often felt so low that she didn't know what to do. I went with her to see the school counsellor. Kerry has been having counselling sessions for a while — she seems to find it easier to see her good qualities now.

All of us encounter difficult challenges in life. Rather than saying, 'I can't do this — I give up,' a young person with healthy self-esteem says, 'I don't understand this — but I'm going to keep trying!'

adolescence The period of life when a child develops into an adult, between the ages of 12 and 20.

airbrushed Altered an image to make it more attractive.

anonymously The act of doing something – writing a letter, posting a comment or tweeting, for example – without saying who you are.

anorexia nervosa A serious eating disorder in which the fear of weight gain leads to eating very little and extreme weight loss.

antisocial Behaving in a manner that is harmful or annoying to other people, or to society in general.

anxiety Fear about something that might happen and your ability to cope with it.

apathy Lack of interest.

bulimia A serious eating disorder in which a person overeats then forces him or herself to vomit.

carbohydrate A compound of carbon, hydrogen and oxygen formed mainly by plants (as sugar, starch or cellulose) – carbohydrates are an important source of energy for the body.

depression A mental state marked by sadness, inactivity and lack of self-esteem.

disruptive Causing a disturbance by interrupting the normal progress of something.

eating disorders Emotional conditions that cause eating habits that are not normal, such as anorexia.

endorphins Chemicals occurring in the brain that can produce a sense of well-being.

foster home A household in which a child is placed to be looked after by people who are not his or her birth parents.

glucose A sugar found in plants and fruit – a source of energy for living things.

hormonal Relating to hormones (chemical substances in the body).

molested Attacked, especially sexually.

phobia A strong, unreasonable fear of something.

puberty The period of life when a young person's sexual organs mature and he or she becomes able to have children.

reckless Showing a lack of care about danger and the possible results of your actions.

resilient The ability to withstand and bounce back from life's knocks.

self-talk A person's inner voice.

stimulant A substance that makes you feel more awake and gives you more energy.

therapist Someone trained to help people deal with mental or emotional problems by talking about those problems.

trauma A very distressing or extreme experience that results in mental or emotional stress or injury.

WEBSITES

epicfriends.co.uk
A website offering help to young people wanting to support friends who are struggling to cope with mental-health issues such as identity, anxiety, bullying and depression.

kidshealth.org/teen
A website offering young people advice on a number of issues, including mental health.

www.rcpsych.ac.uk
The Royal College of Psychiatrists' website. The 'health advice' button leads to parents' and youth information, with help and factsheets for young people.

www.vinspired.com
A charity connecting young people with volunteering opportunities.

www.youngminds.org.uk
A UK charity committed to improving the emotional well-being and mental health of children and young people.

HELPLINES

Childline 0800 1111 www.childline.org.uk

Samaritans 08457 90 90 90 www.samaritans.org

SupportLine 01708 765200 www.supportline.org.uk

BOOKS

The Body Book for Boys, Jonathan Mar, Scholastic Paperbacks, 2010

Body Image and Appearance: The Ultimate Teen Guide, Kathlyn Gay, Scarecrow Press, 2009

How to Feel Good: 20 Things Teens Can Do, Tricia Mangan, Magination Press, 2011

I Just Get So... Angry!: Dealing with Anger and Other Strong Emotions for Teenagers, Timothy Bowden and Sandra Bowden, 2013

The Secret to Teen Power, Paul Harrington, Simon & Schuster Children's, 2009

Teen Esteem: A Self-Direction Manual for Young Adults, Pat Palmer and Melissa Alberti Froehner, Impact Publishers Inc., 2013